Preschool at Home

"What do I do with
my child
before kindergarten?"

Ages 2 - 6

by Debbie Feely

Christian Home Educators Press
595 W. Lambert Road, Suite 101
Brea, CA 92821

Second Edition, 2013

ISBN 978-0-9770707-8-7

Printed in the United States

Table of Contents

Your Preschool Experience

As the new generation of Christian homeschooling parents, you face as great an obstacle as we who came into the movement in the 1980s. Homeschooling is more common and more accepted today, but the culture as a whole is more antagonistic to the Christian lifestyle. Your choice to keep your little ones at home is commendable considering today's political climate claims your child will not succeed without "proper" preschool attendance. Your willingness to take a stand for righteousness is truly a blessing to those who have gone before.

This booklet is designed to give you guidance for the early part of your journey in raising your child to be a successful adult. The ideas and suggestions are presented to help you think through what YOU want for YOUR child. Each section of the booklet has additional resources to help you pursue areas of interest.

Every child is uniquely equipped for God's purpose. As we read in Exodus 31, the Lord tells Moses which men He has prepared for each job in building the tabernacle. Each child develops and learns differently to be prepared for God's unique purpose. In the years between two and six there is often a two-year variance in abilities and readiness to learn certain tasks. This is normal. A child may be quite advanced in one area and yet not in several other areas. We can use these years as a time to teach a love for the Lord and important character traits such as obedience, knowing the child will more easily learn the skills which require a certain degree of readiness when that readiness has been reached. Preschool is the time to build a foundation of faith, values, morals, and manners.

The ideas offered in this booklet should be incorporated into your life in a casual daily manner. If you purpose to be personally involved with your child, watch for teachable moments, and incorporate an atmosphere of discovery into your home, your child will grow and learn. This is true teaching as suggested by Deuteronomy 6:5-7 (NASB):

> You shall love the Lord your God with all your heart, with all your soul, and with all your strength. And these words, which I command you today, shall be in your heart. You shall teach them diligently to your children, and shall talk of them when you sit in your house, when you walk by the way, when you lie down, and when you rise up.

God bless you and your family.

Our Story

When Jerry and I married, we desired to have a God-centered, family-oriented home. After much waiting the Lord granted us two boys, Jeffrey and Robby. We kept them with us as much as possible, and from the beginning worked to disciple and teach them to follow the Lord. In the early '80s, as now, the trend was to encourage early intellectual training. However, we believed children learn best through real life experiences and need to have the opportunity to grow at their own rate without being pressured.

As preschoolers our boys were very different. Jeffrey was a very busy, strong-willed, friendly and exuberant child. His driving thought was, "How does it work?" He learned voraciously, and his constant demand to know more and to try everything kept things moving in our home. He had allergies and at 12 months old began a long battle with ear infections. The damage from these caused perceptual motor difficulties and serious articulation delays. His frustration and resultant behavior caused by his inability to make others understand what he was saying were difficult for all of us. We spent years seeking medical answers.

Robby, on the other hand, was a quiet, observant child. He did not like new experiences and clung closely to his family. When we were out in public, with his hands tightly twined around my neck, I often remembered the counsel I had from a pastor's wife when I was first married. She told me how important it was to allow a clingy child to hold on until he was ready to let go. Robby was a physical child, more interested in doing than knowing. He loved balls of all sorts and every kind of physical challenge. People were always asking, "Is that your little boy up in that tree?"

The boys' differences provide illustrations used with their permission throughout this booklet. This is our story of Jeffrey and Robby's preschool years with a bit of added wisdom.

Making Your Foundation Strong

There is nothing more important in the preschool years than building a strong sense of being a family in Christ. Little children require vast amounts of time and parents find themselves needing to let go of other interests for a season in order to devote time to the children. It is amazing how quickly this time will pass. While you are in the midst of dealing with demanding little ones, it can feel as if it will never end. Use these years to build the kind of family you desire.

Loving God

One of the best things about having your children home with you is the gift of time. There is no need to herd everyone out the door each morning and no rush to fit the day's needs and activities into the evening. This freedom allows plenty of time for sharing God's Word with your children, which in today's busy world is a rare and priceless opportunity.

Some parents read the Bible, even the King James Version, to their preschoolers. Children hearing the King James Version often develop beautiful vocabularies and manners of speech because they have heard them daily.

Other parents read Bible storybooks. We read both. The pictures helped Robby understand what we were reading. Similarly, for memory work, we used Scripture with illustrations such as the Little Golden Book *The Lord is My Shepherd*. With this book, Robby memorized the 23rd Psalm the year he was four (taking most of the year to do so). Scripture Memory Fellowship has lovely illustrated Scripture memory books for preschoolers. Some children can repeat and remember anything they hear, so be in tune with your child's abilities and teach what you can.

It is amazing how much these little ones understand. There is great joy when a child spontaneously joins in prayer for the first time or shows some understanding of salvation. I remember one night when it was my turn for the boys' bedtime routine and evening Bible time. I was reading from a children's book about reconciliation. Six-year-old Jeffrey excitedly said, "I am! I am reconciled to God!" Then I heard a little four-year-old voice say, "Not me, Mommy."

As I taught my children about God, I sometimes forgot I really needed to focus on God. I needed to stay connected to Him in order to have the strength and grace I needed as a parent. I also found I needed to continually go to the Lord with my failings as a parent and to forgive my children for not being the perfect products of my imagination, as I learned to enjoy and appreciate them as God's unique creations.

Your Marriage

As adults, Jeffrey and Robby both have said one of the greatest influences in their lives was having their parents be united in purpose. Robby says that he had advantages as a homeschooler that his non-homeschooled friends did not have. He had the opportunity to be close to his parents and to know his family well. In addition, growing up in a peaceful, loving home provided the foundation for his spiritual growth.

Every three or four months Jerry and I set goals and boundaries for our children. We reviewed them daily so the boys would always hear the same voice from both parents. Although that used to annoy them, now that they are grown, they appreciate that we were consistent.

Jerry and I learned to stand together and support each other through the tough times we had when the boys were little. Walking the floor all night while a toddler sobs in pain is challenging, but the burdens of the death of Jerry's sister and a long-term joblessness were even more difficult. We found support and comfort in the book *Love Life for Every Married Couple* by Ed Wheat.

Your Philosophy

Beginning your homeschool efforts in the preschool years gives you the opportunity to understand a Christian worldview and to develop a philosophy of education. In other words, you can take this time to learn how to think in a way that is consistent with scripture. This is particularly true for those raised in non-Christian homes and public school backgrounds.

Your worldview is the way you understand God, man, and man's relationship to God, and must be based on the truth of Scripture. God's Word and your worldview affect the choices you make in your daily life. One day our family realized the impact of this when Jeffrey (as many five year olds do) developed a fascination for dinosaurs and we had no biblically based answers to the questions about where dinosaurs fit into the framework of God's creation. We found we needed to find specific answers that fit with Scripture and to let go of some beliefs that were prevalent in our culture.

For another example, today we are told it takes a village to raise a child, that a child is a product of the culture and needs the government to happy and well adjusted. We, however, believe every child is God's unique and special creation, created for His glory and honor, loaned to parents as a precious gift for a season, and that God chose parents not government for the special task of raising the child, making the family and not the government the first order of society.

Philosophy is the explanation of the underlying reasons of various disciplines. Theology and ethics are both branches of philosophy, providing explanations of what we believe about God and about human behavior. When we undertake to train and teach our children at home it is important to formulate a philosophy of education.

Some of the questions relating to academic studies that we thought about during the preschool years included: How do children learn best? What makes the best atmosphere for children to grow and thrive, including the issue of TV? What place do our Christian beliefs have in education? We believed from the beginning that children learn best through real life experiences.

We decided that children should be allowed to discover areas of interest and to move ahead in areas of strength while being gently coached in areas where they struggle. Thus, Robby was able to multiply and divide before he recognized the alphabet. Our philosophy of child training and education is discussed further throughout this booklet.

In this postmodern era in which absolutes are mocked, it becomes more important to filter all thought through Scripture. If you spend time reading a variety of books about education, homeschooling, and worldview, you will know what you believe and why, what it is you want to teach your children, and how you want to teach them.

Parent helps:

- The Gesell Institute Child Development Series by Louise Bates Ames and Frances Ilg
- *A Biblical Psychology of Learning* by Dr. Ruth Beechick
- *How to Really Love Your Child* by Ross Campbell
- *Disciplines of a Godly Family* by Kent and Barbara Hughes
- *For the Children's Sake* by Susan Schaeffer Macaulay
- *Parents' Guide to the Spiritual Growth of Children* by Rick Osborne and John Trent
- CHEA's Firm Foundation Library:
  Homeschooling from a Biblical Worldview, by Israel Wayne
  Homeschooling, The Right Choice, by Christopher Klicka
  Let Us Highly Resolve, by David and Shirley Quine
  Encyclopedia of Bible Truths, by Ruth Haycock

Building Your Child's Foundation

Training your child to be obedient, respectful, and mannerly is not only biblical; it is so exceptional these days that others will notice. The well-behaved, mannerly child is one who stands out and earns the respect of others.

Obedience

Before you correct a child's behavior, the child needs an understanding of what is expected. Teach your child that obedience means doing what they are told to do when they are told to do it. Obedience also means doing what is right, even if no one is watching you and Mommy is not there to tell you what to do. As your child becomes older you will find the time spent teaching obedience during the preschool years will make academic lessons, the times you spend out in public, and the little things, such as allowing your child to play out front, far easier on everyone. The Scriptures are full of examples of the consequences of not obeying, providing an excellent resource for teaching the concept.

Give a direction just once in your normal tone of voice. If your child does not obey, firmly but calmly, and in a friendly manner, enforce your directions. Soon first-time obedience will be learned. Of course, it is polite if your child is immersed in a project to give a few minutes notice that a change is coming. Some children have difficulty with change and transition, so a warning is helpful. However, be careful not to allow delays to become a way for your child to postpone obedience.

Jerry used to say to me, "Don't just say it, get up and make sure they are doing what you say." Training in obedience takes work. Overlooking minor disobediences seems easier, but has undesirable consequences. The child will either continue to test and push you, or will become confused and fearful, not knowing where the boundaries are. An obedient child is a secure child.

I used to think that when Jeffrey was happy, he was like Christmas, the Fourth of July, and Disneyland, all at once. When he was not happy, he was like a hurricane. On the other hand, when Robby was happy, he was like a picnic on a sunny day in April. When he was not happy, he reminded me of a drippy faucet. It took several friends and family members to point out that while we dealt with Jeff's exuberance, Robby was quietly becoming a bratty child. Then we realized, whether children are outspoken or quiet, they need to be guided to a right attitude in their heart. We found the guidance we needed in James Dobson's "A Checklist for Spiritual Training," included at the end of this booklet.

Sibling Rivalry

Sibling rivalry is a concern for many families. My mother's tried and true method for dealing with five fussing children was to require us to sit together on the sofa until we were ready to be friends. I had Jeffrey and Robby sit on the entryway step. It rarely took more than three minutes for them to be laughing together. Timeout together is far more effective than separation. A child may fuss and squabble when hungry, tired, or just needing some loving attention. A snuggle on the sofa with a story, or a quiet time for him to share his heart are ways to restore your child to good humor.

Respect

Respect is recognizing and honoring others. This attitude comes from routinely modeling good manners and having a servant's heart in your home. It helps if you teach what is expected of your child at home, such as using a napkin or holding the door for his elders. This practice saves your child from being embarrassed. Your child should learn to speak respectfully, as the result of a respectful heart. This includes learning to honor people of all ages (with special respect for older adults), finding ways to be helpful, and appreciating help received. Your child will grow in this area as you recognize and say thank you for the efforts to be helpful.

Teach your child to respect and admire Mommy and Daddy by modeling that respect and admiration. Daddy becomes his son's role model and his daughter's hero in part because Mom teaches the children to defer to Daddy as the head of their home. When Daddy treats Mommy as his greatest treasure, the children share that attitude. Think about ways to enhance the love and respect in your home.

Learning through Daily Life

Daily life offers many opportunities for teaching your child. You have already done this from the moment of birth, teaching to hold still while you change his diapers, to put on clothes independently, to put toys in the basket, to not touch the hot stove, and more. Involving your child in your daily routine gives your child a sense of belonging and pride in his family and home.

The suggestions given in each section are only the beginning. You will have ideas of your own and there are many sources to give you even more ideas.

Schedules

Children are more comfortable with routine in the home. An easy way to begin is to have Bible time after breakfast and before bedtime. Add a rest time after lunch and you have a routine. We did Bible time after breakfast because Robby always woke up crying for his Cheerios®. You and your children may find that another sequence works better for you, and you may want more or less of a routine. Because each family is different due to the parent's work hours, the children's sleeping habits, and other demands, there is no one way to devise a schedule. However, it helps if you stay home as often as possible and have some sort of regularity to your day.

Chores

Teaching routine household chores is an excellent way to teach obedience. Chores have immediate rewards; when you wash the dishes they are clean. A child learns the benefits of doing what needs to be done and the value of effort, and will begin to understand that effort produces results be beginning formal lessons. A child can do most household chores by the age of six, although not as well as an adult. Having children for housekeepers means your home may not be as clean as you would like, and teaching and training takes more time than doing it yourself. However, having children who know how to work hard, work as a team, and contribute something valuable and real to the household is worth the patience. Thirty minutes a day spent cleaning together will help you stay on top of the work.

You can teach chores by the tried and true discipleship method: First, you do it while your child observes. Then, you talk the child through the chore. Next, the child talks you through the chore.

Next, the child does the chore while you observe. Finally, the child does the chore alone. Each of these steps will need to be repeated and retraining will be necessary as the child matures and is able to do the job more thoroughly

Children are overwhelmed by big jobs. If their bedroom is knee deep in things, help the children get the job done by coaching them. "Find all the blue things and pick them up." It will make a big difference if you get things organized and reduce the amount of things in a room so the job is not so big. It is hard for children to put things away if the drawers are filled to overflowing.

Snacks

Snack time makes a great learning time. Your children can practice pouring if they have a small pitcher. They will enjoy stacking crackers with cheese or adding raisins to peanut butter on crackers or celery, eventually learning to spread the peanut butter as well. By the time children are five they can make a lunch of sandwiches for the family. Preschoolers enjoy helping with baking, especially licking spoons and washing up the utensils. Of course you will not want the mess and bother every snack time, but give your child the opportunity to do as much as he is able. There are many cute children's cookbooks available to give you ideas.

Because Jeffrey needed to eat often, snack time was important for us. Your child may not need to eat snacks; they could interfere with healthy eating at mealtime. Some children seem to barely eat, but if you avoid sweets and other empty foods they will eat what they need. Do what is best for your child.

Rest Time

Rest time is helpful for both you and your child even without napping. A quiet time of 30 minutes gives Mom a chance to rest and the child will relax and unwind as well. This time also teaches the child to focus on quiet activities, and more importantly it gives a bit of time to think. Jerry always said the boys needed to have quiet time so they could hear the voice of the Lord. He felt it was important for children to spend time without any media input.

Play Time

If you include your children in your daily routine and give them basic tools to play with, you will see them acting out what they are learning and imitating the adults around them. Consider how much more benefit children get from imitating real people and good books, rather than playing with popular TV-based toys. We looked for things that would allow our boys to use their own imagination. Jerry once gave the boys a set of PVC pipes of different lengths with an assortment of joints. They made everything from corrals to trombones to guns with them.

Playtime for little children is a learning time and needs to be seen as such. It is their "work" time. With appropriate real-life tools, children will keep themselves busy, applying and internalizing the things they are learning. When children are expected to play with "toys" they quickly become bored, whiny, and aimless.

Suggested play tools:

- Buckets and paintbrushes for painting with water
- Shovels and other garden tools for digging and making mud
- Building blocks and/or plastic, snap together bricks
- Toy cars and other vehicles
- Simple no-name dolls or stuffed animals with clothing
- Hammers and other tools
- Child-size brooms, toy kitchens with equipment, and other household role-playing toys
- Modeling clay using tools such as cookie cutters
- Balls of different types
- Dress up clothes for playing pretend
- Large squares of fabric for creating costumes
- Puppets
- Large pieces of something for pretend, such as cardboard boxes
- A bed sheet or two for forts or playhouses
- Chalkboard or white board
- Puzzles

- Bible felts or other felt sets

Physical Activity

Competence in movement is essential for the proper development of perceptual motor skills. Perceptual motor development is the specific process by which one takes in information from the senses, organizes and interprets that information in the brain, and then responds to it. The response should be automatic and instantaneous. This ability allows a child to be successful academically and socially. Some guided physical activity for preschoolers insures that they are developing the motor skills they need to succeed.

Children usually enjoy active play times. Observing your child and frequently offering a few challenges, you will ensure needed large motor development. For example you can challenge your child by suggesting that lines can be drawn in various patterns and can be used for hopscotch and other games. The one-on-one attention and companionship is reason enough to engage your child in active games. When children get bored and begin to squabble, it is effective to offer them a physical challenge such as having everyone hop around the table or prance like a pony across the yard.

Activities:

- Stand against a wall with head back and bend side to side.
- Walk on tiptoes.
- Walk on a straight line.
- Draw large circles in the air.
- Crawl with opposite hand and knee moving together.
- Crab walk, left-hand right-foot, right-hand left-foot.
- Do angels in the snow, slowly moving limbs together and in opposition.
- March like a soldier.
- Jump on two feet. Hop on each foot. Play hopscotch. Jump like a frog.
- Catch a ball, toss a ball, bounce a ball. Toss and catch a beanbag. Toss beanbags to a target.
- Play tetherball and jump rope.
- Generally give your child many opportunities to jump, run, hop, skip, climb, crawl, ride, bounce, and swing.

Read Aloud

The benefits of reading aloud to your child are many. It creates a sense of family unity and togetherness while building a cultural worldview. The books you choose to read aloud will influence your child's views of the way things are. As the child listens auditory memory is developed. As you read chapter books, which require remembering from one day to the next, you help improve your child's long-term memory. Listening also gives the child a framework for learning independent reading.

Each child reacts differently while listening to stories. Jeffrey was listening to chapter books such as the original *Winnie the Pooh* by A. A. Milne by the time he was two. Robby, on the other hand, only liked to look at the pictures. His favorite was *Goodnight Moon* by Margaret Wise Brown; we "read" it by looking for the pictures of the balloon. Since I read aloud everyday, Robby did hear quite a bit, although I did not require either boy to sit while I read. They often played quietly on the floor while they listened. I knew they were listening by their response.

Honey for a Child's Heart by Gladys Hunt is a great guide for finding good books to read to your preschooler. Mrs. Hunt says, "A good book has a profound kind of morality not a cheap, sentimental sort which thrives on shallow plots and superficial heroes, but the sort of force which inspires the reader's inner life and draws out all that is noble. A good writer has something worthy to say and says it in the best possible way. Then he respects the child's ability to understand. Principles are not preached but are implicit in the writing."[1]

Favorite preschool books:

- *Mother Goose* (Try taking several versions from the library at once and discussing the difference in the illustrations.)
- *Madeline* by Ludwig Bemelmans

- *Mike Mulligan and His Steam Shovel* and others by Virginia Burton
- *The Story of Babar the Little Elephant* and series by Jean and Laurent de Brunhoff
- *Are You My Mother*?, and others by PD Eastman
- *The Story about Ping* and others by Marjorie Flack
- *Millions of Cats* by Wanda Gag
- *Where's Spot* by Eric Hill
- *What Do You Do, Dear?* and *What Do You Say, Dear?* by Sesyle Joslin
- *Jump, Frog, Jump* by Robert Kalan
- *Whose Mouse Are You?*, *Leo the Late Bloomer,* and others by Robert Kraus
- *Fish is Fish* and others by Leo Lionni
- *Make Way for Ducklings* and others by Robert McCloskey
- *Mousekin's ABC* and series by Edna Miller
- *The Little Wood Duck* by Brian Wildsmith
- *Harry the Dirty Dog* by Gene Zion

Learning through Activities

Special activities are sometimes called enrichment. I call them fun. These ideas are things you personally enjoy and choose to do with your child. My mother loved to sit and make us tiny animals from modeling cay. She also spent time coloring with us. Jeffery and I enjoyed building with Lego® bricks together. I also enjoyed anything that got us all outside and involved with nature whether it was digging in the dirt at home or hiking in the mountains. Parents will have unique ideas and interests to share with their children.

Again, look at the suggestions with each section as only the beginning. Ideas are everywhere.

Music

Your preschooler may enjoy recording stories and songs with a recorder or computer. This leads to hours of fun and giggles. Traditional children's songs, Scripture set to music, worship songs, hymns, and any music that you like may be enjoyed on CDs or MP3s.

We had fun with the "Wee Sing" book and cassette sets. These recordings include all the standard classic songs that children typically learn. Their popularity is shown by the continual release of new sets.

Those of you with musical talents will be able delve into music further. Our boys were involved in our church music ministry with their father from the time they were preschoolers, and today they both have a love for music and worship. Also, Jerry often played the piano at night while the boys were falling asleep. See how you can incorporate music into your home.

Arts and Crafts

Your child needs opportunities to use arm and shoulder muscles to develop the proper neural pathways that will help in learning the fine motor skill of writing. A child who has not learned to use these muscles will isolate the skill of writing to fingers only, causing a white-knuckle grip on the pencil while writing, leading to fatigue. Painting with water on the fence or on the patio is one way to develop large muscle motor skills. Drawing with sidewalk chalk is another way. Your local newspaper gives away, or sells for a nominal cost, roll ends of paper wide enough for drawing large pictures.

Other fun projects include

- stringing cereal or macaroni. Shoelaces work

well because they have a stiff end.
- cutting freehand to learn to use scissors. Increase the difficulty by drawing broad lines on paper with markers. Begin with straight lines, followed by increasingly complex lines.
- playing with Play-Doh® helps develop dexterity as the child learns to roll snakes or balls.
- dipping the wheels of a little car in paint and driving it across the paper.

Craft supplies:

- Paper of various kinds and weights
- Crayons, markers, and pencils
- Play-Doh®
- Glue of various kinds
- Scissors
- Paints
- Starch for finger painting
- Pipe cleaners

Resources:

- *I Can Make a Rainbow* by Marjorie Frank
- *Puddles and Wings and Grapevine Swings* by Imogene Forte and Marjorie Frank

Science

Of the numerous reasons for doing science activities with your children, the foremost is to help them see God through His creation. Through the patterns in leaves, the intricacies of snowflakes, the abundance of sand at the seashore, and the stars in the sky, our children see the greatness of their Creator and the way His hand upholds it all. Through science, children also learn thinking skills, observation and deduction, and cause and effect. In her book *Five Homespun Steps for Teaching Your Child to Read*, Dr. Ruth Beechick tells about a study comparing how two groups of kindergarten children learned to read. One group was taught intensive reading while the other group spent equal time learning science, with no formal reading lessons. By the third grade, the science group was reading more effectively because they had better vocabularies and better thinking skills, learned from the science lessons.[2]

Outdoor science activities:

- Go on expeditions often; a walk around the block is a great adventure for two- to four-year-olds. If you make some binoculars out of toilet paper rolls and a hat out of newspaper, you have a safari. Look for trails of ants, falling leaves, birds, different types of flowers, and more.
- Plant seeds and bulbs, or put seeds on a damp sponge and watch them sprout.
- Take apart various flowers to see how they are made.
- Place various leaves under paper and rub them with a crayon to make their shapes and veins.
- Put a caterpillar and a tomato plant branch into a

jar with dirt in the bottom. The caterpillar will pupate and come out as a moth or butterfly.

- If you live near a stream, play Pooh sticks: Stand on a bridge and drop a stick into the water then rush to the other side to see the stick float by.
- Make mud pies.
- Grow a huge sunflower.
- Play with the hose and dig holes.
- Get flashlights out and lay on a blanket in the yard at night, looking at stars.
- Discover the world God made.

Indoor science activities:

- Boil water and see the steam. Hold a clear glass dish in the steam and watch the steam condense.
- Put water into the freezer in a plastic container and see that the water gets bigger as it freezes.
- Take two balloons and blow one up. Fasten the balloons to each end of a yardstick. Balance the stick. Which balloon is heaviest?
- Make paper airplanes.
- Buy liquids in half pint, pint, quart, half gallon, and gallon containers. Use the containers in the tub to learn about measuring.
- Mix equal measures of cornstarch and water to make a gooey mess that solidifies and liquefies in amazing ways when you squish it in your hands.
- Play with magnets to see what they will stick to.

Field Trips

A trip to the market is a field trip for your preschooler, as is a trip to the post office, the doctor, the polling place, and any other place you frequent. You can think of it as learning about "My Community." Rather than leaving him home with your spouse or babysitter, take your child, using the trip as a teaching opportunity. At the market, work on learning the names of the vegetables and talk about where things come from. Robby enjoyed going to a plant nursery where he chose his own rose bush, as a gift from his grandma. You may want to ask your dentist if your child can visit and see all the equipment before going in for an appointment. The more things a child knows personally, the easier it will be to read and be able to put a word with a reality.

If possible, take regular trips to visit daddy at work. Not only will your child enjoy seeing what daddy does all day, but also it will help him begin to understand the world of work.

The idea of field trips may lead you to ask, "Don't we need a group to do a field trip?" As mentioned previously, any outing is a learning experience for your child. On the other hand, there are some things that are fun to do with a group. For preschool, two or three moms and their children make a group. You can take your group to the zoo, the fire station, a local bakery, and many other places. Just call and ask before you go if it is not a place that is open to the public. Jeffrey loved fire trucks and was so excited when we visited a real fire station with another family. The boys were able to see how the trucks work and try on a real fire hat.

Playgroups

Beginning when Jeffrey was about a year old and for the next few years, we participated in a playgroup. Jeff and I, and later Robby, met with two or three other mothers and their children at a park for about an hour each week. A play group may be as simple as that or you may do something such as taking turns meeting in each other's homes where each mother plans a special activity such as playing in a rhythm band or decorating cookies.

Later when we discovered homeschooling, we found several like-minded families and met with them at various times for meals, birthday celebrations, special activities, and outings. Having the dads be involved was fun and provided our children with an "extended" family Jerry and I did not have in our town. A playgroup can serve many types of needs. You need only find one or two like-minded families to begin.

Learning Academic Skills

Academic skills are addressed last because they are the least important of all that your child learns as a preschooler. A few children will make it clear that they are ready to learn some academic skills but, as I have said before, it can be done in a casual informal way. If your child wants to make a picture for grandma and then asks how to write I love you, you can demonstrate how to write *I love you.* You do not need formal lessons at this age.

Math Concepts

When you set the table, you can say to your child, "We have four family members. Count and lay out four forks." This teaches one-to-one correspondence. Look for other ways to count.

An analog clock that has a second hand and the minutes marked is a great tool for teaching time. You can also make a clock face from a paper plate, a brad, and hands cut out of another paper plate. Talk about time and show your preschooler how to move the clock hands. Telling time comes slowly; some preschoolers can tell the hour, but many cannot. Every evening when Jeffrey was small I would say, "Look, Jeff, the big hand is up and the little hand is down, it is six o'clock and time for daddy to come home."

"More than," "less than," and fractions are easily taught with cookies.

Circles, squares, and triangles are the shapes typically learned by preschoolers, but why not learn more? We played "find the shape" often. I would say, "Do you see anything in this room that has the shape of a circle?" As the game went on for several years, Jeffrey and Robby learned to name spheres and cylinders and more.

Four year olds can learn to draw a cross, a circle, and a square, but drawing diagonal lines often doesn't come until about age five.

As with any concept, matching is a good way to learn colors. "Here is a red sock. Can you find another red sock?" As the matches are made, your child is also learning the concept of sets. If you have Lego® bricks or pattern blocks or any other colorful small items, put all the same colors together. Then learn sequencing: red, yellow, blue, red, yellow, blue; continue the pattern. After some practice following the patterns you make, your child can begin to make up the repeating sequences.

Numerals can be taught with flash cards. Have the child lay out number cards, beginning with 1 through 5, and practice putting the correct number of beans or other small items on each card. Once a child recognizes that the Arabic numeral 4 means a quantity of four objects you can play games such as the old family board game Sorry®. Using only one game piece, have the child draw the numeral and move the game piece the correct amount of spaces. Most family games can be adapted to preschool use, so there is no reason to buy preschool games.

Measure many things and talk about inches, feet, and yards, but do not expect your child to use these accurately at this age. Cut sandwiches in half and in quarters, and talk about parts as fractions.

Language

Reading is about language. If children learn to read by rote without learning the richness of language, they never learn to enjoy reading for the sake of hearing the music of words. When you read poetry, memorize nursery rhymes, and sing nursery songs and finger plays such as "Itsy Bitsy Spider," you are enhancing your child's understanding of the way words work. Be aware that rhyming is developmental; suddenly, at about age four, a child can rhyme, but probably not before that age. Encourage your preschooler to tell you stories. Then write the story in a book made of sheets of paper folded into a book shape and covered with construction paper. Your child will enjoy illustrating the book

Bible story felts are another way to encourage your child to tell stories.

Your child will enjoy hearing you tell stories. Favorites are ones about themselves. You can tell a bedtime a story about what was done during the day or a special story about your child's birth or other exciting events. These are stories that will be requested over and over.

When you read a story, stop and ask, "What do you think is going to happen next?"

Talk about calendars: months of the year, days of the week, and birthdays, but do not expect your child to use these correctly.

Help your child learn full name, address, and phone number, and mommy and daddy's names. Again recognize this is a long-term project.

Resources:

- *Language and Thinking for Young Children* by Ruth Beechick

Reading

Children are very different when it comes to learning to read. Jeffrey's grandma gave him a tray of magnetic letters for his second birthday, and he quickly learned the names of all the letters by using it as a puzzle. By the time he was five, he knew all the letter sounds, and we played a game where he would draw a letter card and name a word that began or ended with that sound. When we began "reading lessons" for kindergarten, he quickly began to read.

Robby did not learn the names of the letters at two or three or four or five. By then I was worried, but everyone urged me not to compare him to his brother. Robby did not learn all the letters consistently without mixing up similar shapes until he was eight. He went on to achieve well; he just did it later. On the other hand, my daughter-in-law, Deborah, began reading on her own at age three by listening to her brother being taught to read. Beginning to read has nothing to do with intelligence but rather with personal developmental timing.

Prepare your child for reading by reading aloud. Look at the way books work: they all open the same way, have a beginning, middle, and end, as well as a title, an author, and sometimes an illustrator. As you read many books, even your two-year-old will find favorites. Then when you go to the library, you can point out, for instance, that Frank Ashe bear books can be found at the beginning of the row with an "A" on the spine of the book.

While you read aloud, show your child how the sentences proceed from left to right across the page by moving your finger under the sentence. As learning letters begins, and later words, stop and point them out in the book. If your child has learned that c-a-t is cat, find a book about cats. Point to each word as you read the book, and when you come to the word cat, your child can read it.

Most children love to hear the same books over and over. This repetition is good preparation for learning to read because as they memorize the story, it will help them figure out how to decipher the printed words.

Once your child has learned the upper case

and lower case letter names, you can teach matching uppers to lowers. A set of alphabet flash cards or rubber ABC puzzles can be used to teach letters.

How do you know if a child is ready to read? You will be asked, “What does this say?” as well as pointing out, spelling out, and even trying to sound out various signs and words seen both at home and around town. Children “pretend” to read from favorite books. At this point some children actually are reading. They have picked up enough clues and heard a story often enough to put together the reading code on their own and simply begin to read.

If your child is four or five, knows the names of the letters, and seems to be trying to read independently, you may want to begin to use some phonics lessons. Keep the lesson to a maximum of 10 to 15 minutes a day, if the child is willing and interested. This is not the time to push. If a child is really ready to read, simply introduce letter sounds a few at a time and show how the sounds blend (c-a-t says cat). This will be enough to learn how words work.

The most important thing to remember about teaching reading is that preschoolers do not need to learn to read. If ready to read, they will do it on their own with no help at all. Otherwise, nearly all children catch up to the same reading level at about age 10, regardless of when they begin.

Additional Helps

Frequently Asked Questions

What about socialization?

God put children into families as their primary social circle. When we consider that it is our goal to raise responsible adults, we can ask, "Who is best suited to be the role model or hero for my three-year-old: another three-year-old or Daddy?" Recent studies show that homeschool graduates are successful as adults. More than 70 percent participate in elections and in church and other social institutions compared to less than 30 percent of those who were not homeschooled. The National Home Education Research Institute (NHERI) and Home School Legal Defense Association (HSLDA) have informational booklets with more details on homeschool success.

Resources

- *Home Educated and Now Adults* by Brian D.

Ray, Ph.D., National Home Education Research Institute (www.nheri.org).

- For free brochures with homeschool statistics, contact Home School Legal Defense Association, www.hslda.org.

But shouldn't my child go to a preschool for the experience and then homeschool later?

Many people ask this and I truly believe children should *not* go to preschool. I remember when I was helping at our church preschool before Jeffrey was born, a teacher with a master's degree in early childhood education told me it would be better for my child if I kept him home. We did try Mommy and Me preschool when Jeffrey was four, at the advice of a counselor who was helping us with his speech difficulties, and while the program was a good one, I felt all we gained was the knowledge that there were bigger and better toys that we did not own. An article from Austega's Gifted Services in Australia suggests placing gifted children in a preschool setting may even be detrimental because teachers and other students will not know how to deal with their differences.[3]

How do I find a homeschool group?

Check the Homeschool Directory at the Christian Home Educators Association of California website (www.cheaofca.org) or call 562-864-2432 for groups in California or organizations in other states.

What about allowances?

Preschoolers do not have much understanding of what money means. You may want to consider giving your child money for the church offering, but it isn't until about age six that children seem to become interested in money.

What about MY time?

Sometimes there are doctor appointments or other errands that are difficult to do with children. My friend Judy and I solved this by watching each other's children. One Tuesday afternoon, Josh and Keiko would come to our house; the next week, Jeffrey and Robby would go to their house. That gave us each two afternoons a month to have a lunch out and do the things we needed to do without the children.

It really helps Mom if every day you have your children rest, whether they nap or not. Even an active four year old will benefit from a quiet half-hour on the bed looking at books. Then Mom gets a bit of time to be quiet and alone to regroup for the rest of the day.

My child is gifted, what can I do?

The reality is that God gifts all children for His purposes. I was pleased to discover as I read through goals and objectives for gifted children that some homeschool materials assume ALL children should be taught as though they are gifted, encouraging them to find and develop areas of interest, and to advance in areas where they are more able.

If your child is truly academically gifted, encourage learning, but do not expect your child to do schoolwork that is beyond the appropriate developmental age. In other words, a four-year-old reading at a second-grade level does not mean being ready to do second-grade schoolwork or to act like a second grader. A preschooler should not be expected to sit as long or do as much pencil work as a second grader. Allow as much reading as your child wants to within reason, but let your preschooler be a preschool child. Give your child the opportunity to learn without needing to move forward too soon. However, you can't assume academic giftedness because your child reads at a young age. Some children just have a unique ability to discover codes. In the same way many very bright children read later than average or have learning disabilities.

When a friend asked what she should do since her three year old was already reading, the head of the gifted and talented education program in her area wisely told her, “If your child is academically gifted, he will still be academically gifted when he is 10 or 12. Right now, he needs to be a little kid. Teach him social skills such as how to get along with people and how to use good manners. Then let him play.”

My child has special needs, what can I do?

Physical or mental impairment

If your child has special needs you probably have a team of specialists working with you to enhance your child's opportunities for growth or for life itself. Your choice to keep your child at home may concern the people, who are involved with your special services, but other families have their special children at home and support and encouragement is available. It will be helpful to speak to Home School Legal Defense Association's special needs specialist for help in knowing how to coordinate your parental rights with the outside help you may need.

Learning disabilities

Because there is such a wide range of developmental rates among young children there is probably no need to be concerned about learning disabilities at this point. It can be helpful to raise your concerns with your pediatrician such as when we asked if Jeff was hyperactive and were assured he was not. If your heart tells you there is something not quite right bring it to the Lord and trust Him to direct you to the right help at the right time. Milder problems may be discounted by professionals until the child is considerably older, again because there is a two or more year variance in learning at this stage and by most definitions a child must lag more than two years behind developmental norms to be labeled as learning disabled. You may want to think through whether you want a label for your child.

Resources:

- National Challenged Homeschoolers Associated Network (NATHHAN) has a newsletter, products, and people with experience, who can encourage you as you work with your child. Contact NATHHAN at 208.267.6246 (www.nathhan.com).
- Almaden Valley Christian School (AVCS) offers materials useful for teaching children with special needs, and a consulting service, although they usually have a waiting list. Contact AVCS at 408.997.0290 (www.almadenvalleychristianschool.com).

What if my child needs speech therapy?

Some delays in articulation, or the ability to pronounce specific sounds, is developmental and will correct itself as the child grows older. Other areas of speech development include being able to express ideas and being able to understand the speech of others. If you have concerns about any of these areas ask your pediatrician.

NATHHAN (see previous section) has speech programs for use at home, including *Straight Talk* 1 and 2, which are reasonably priced and may be all you need. Some speech pathologists will work with the parent, meeting about once a month to assign new goals and to demonstrate what needs to be done.

Will my child be able to go to college if we homeschool?

Probably. This isn't something you can determine while your child is so young. Homeschooled students do attend many top ranking colleges, but as the political and cultural climate grows more negative towards Christian beliefs some of that may change. A better question may be will homeschooling allow my child to grow in God's unique and created ways?

Are you a real homeschooler?

Yes. We first heard about homeschooling when Jeffrey was five. Homeschooling was an idea that fit our chosen lifestyle and worked well for our family. It was not always easy. Sometimes I wanted to give up but Jerry was faithful to what he believed was best for our children and encouraged me. For the most part the boys were happy at home. There was a time when Jeffrey thought he would like to attend the local public high school so we prayed about it and as we did he realized he would lose a lot of freedom by being tied to a campus all day. When Robby was 12 he said we had ruined his life by making him different from his friends. Today, having survived those peer-influenced teen years, he is thankful he was taught at home. We taught the boys at home for 13 years. They went on to college and now Jeffrey is married and working as a computer systems integrator and Rob is studying for the ministry. We all believe homeschooling was the best choice for our family.

A Checklist for Spiritual Training

by Dr. James Dobson

Concept I: "And thou shalt love the Lord thy God with all thy heart." Mark 12:30

- Is your child learning of the love of God through the love, tenderness, and mercy of his parents? (most important)
- Is he learning to talk about the Lord, and to include Him in his thoughts and plans? Is he learning to turn to Jesus for help whenever he is frightened or anxious or lonely? Is he learning to read the Bible?
- Is he learning to pray?
- Is he learning the joy of the Christian way of life?
- Is he learning the meaning of faith and trust?
- Is he learning the beauty of Jesus' birth and death?

Concept II: "Thou shalt love thy neighbor as thyself." Mark 12:31

- Is he learning to understand and empathize with the feelings of others?
- Is he learning not to be selfish and demanding?
- Is he learning to share?
- Is he learning not to gossip and criticize others?
- Is he learning to accept himself?

Concept III: "Teach me to do thy will; for thou art my God." Psalm 145:10

- Is he learning to obey his parents as preparation for later obedience to God? (most important)
- Is he learning to behave properly in church, God's house?
- Is he learning healthy appreciation for both aspects of God's nature: love and justice?
- Is he learning that there are many forms of benevolent authority outside himself to which he must submit?
- Is he learning the meaning of sin and its inevitable consequences?

Concept IV: "Fear God and keep His commandments; for this is the whole duty of man." Ecclesiastes 12:13

- Is he learning to be truthful and honest?
- Is he learning to keep the Sabbath day holy?
- Is he learning the relative insignificance of materialism?
- Is he learning the meaning of the Christian family, and the faithfulness to it which God intends?
- Is he learning to follow the dictates of his own conscience?

Concept V: "But the Fruit of the Spirit is. . .self-control." Galatians 5:22-23

- Is he learning to give a portion of his allowance and other money to God?
- Is he learning to control his impulses?
- Is he learning to work and carry responsibility?
- Is he learning the vast difference between self-

worth and egotistical pride?
•Is he to bow in reverence before the God of the universe?

Works Cited

1 Hunt, Gladys, *Honey for a Child's Heart*, 3rd ed., Michigan: Zondervan, 1989.

2 Beechick, Ruth, *Five Homespun Steps for Teaching Your Child to Read,* USA: Arrow Press, 1985.

4 Farmer, David, *Parenting Gifted Preschoolers*, www.austega.com/gifted/16-gifted/articles/16-parenting-giftedpreschoolers.html

Additional Resources

Barnier, Carol, *The Big WHAT NOW Book of Learning Styles*
Beechick, Dr. Ruth, *A Biblical Home Education*
Heart and Mind: What the Bible Says About Learning
Bendt, Valerie, *Making the Most of the Preschool years: 100 Activities to Encourage Independent Play*
Plowman, Ginger, *Don't Make Me Count to Three*
Ronney, Karen, *Proud Parents Guide to Raising Athletic, Balanced, and Coordinated*
Tobias, Cynthia, *The Way They Learn*

AWANA
www.awana.org

The Disciple Curriculum
www.thedisciplecurriculum.com

Doorpost parenting and character training materials
www.doorposts.com

SEEDS Family Worship CDs
www.seedsmusicstore.com

www.ingramcontent.com/pod-product-compliance
Lightning Source LLC
Chambersburg PA
CBHW071644040426
42452CB00009B/1751